This is a Love Song

For Sandra, who is everywhere in this book and in my life.

This is a Love Song

HUGH MACDONALD

Black Moss Press
2011

Cataloguing In Publication (CIP) data for this book is available through The Canadian CIP Program coordinated by Library and Archives Canada.

ISBN: 978-0-88753-486-7

Cover photo: Cherie Marion

Layout & cover design: Jasmine Elliott

 **Black Moss Press**

Published by Black Moss Press at 2450 Byng Road, Windsor, Ontario, N8W 3E8. Canada. Black Moss books are distributed in Canada and the U.S. by LitDistCo. All orders should be directed there.

Black Moss would like to acknowledge the generous financial support from both the Canada Council of the Arts and the Ontario Arts Council.

 Canada Council   Conseil des Arts
for the Arts   du Canada

 ONTARIO ARTS COUNCIL
CONSEIL DES ARTS DE L'ONTARIO

PRINTED IN CANADA

Contents

Geese

Brudenell, PE Nov 27

Beyond the south-faced river windows
the deck sits damp, a skim of pocked ice
melts softly from its Wolmanized floor.
Yesterday's expanse of snow-laden lawn
reclaims its pale green garb of faded summer:
cupped pale leaves strewn like pie-crust shells
unraked remnants of the autumnal décor,
the reds and yellows of drowsy maple and aspen
strewn here and there, knots on an antique quilt.
Now skeletal, arms like posing ballerinas,
the trees alert and naked in this winter thaw
profiled against a silken haze that hides
away the world beyond the lawn's horizon.
I sit at our table, lost in Follett's Whiteout,
sip comfortably on the day's best cup of tea
when sudden telltale honks of fleeing geese
left to right, east to west, sound their approach.
I raise my eyes above the trees to watch ...
instead like strafing fighter jets they swoop,
dark shapes skim by in a grey soup dawn
at the earth's edge where water ought to flow,
ghosts pierce the murky morning river fog.
They pass, explode upon my absent-minded calm,
then fade like a million unspoken memories.

In October's Fountain

The woman in October's fountain by the canal, in the city square opposite Lord Elgin's Hotel, may be no perfect beauty, yet her pretty face hints awareness of what water does to cotton cloth, and that passers-by will likely look, and note that beneath her blouse she wears no bra. Her photographer has the gear he needs for this playful romp in the park. His pants summer short, his smart runners idle beside her chic boots, his cases and bags. We had been shopping at the Rideau Centre, my energetic, pretty wife of many years and I, tote what we've bought, and scorching cups from the tiny Starbucks there, where we failed to find a spot to sit and sip, and opted thus to rest 'mid fountain mists and autumn leaves. At first we sense our plan diminished by this scene. We almost walk away, embarrassed to be taken for voyeurs, but shrug, and stay instead, drink while our coffee's hot. We sip and chat, while spell-bound passers-by gather, crowding close in startled awe as this girl shivers into shallow leaf-strewn water, floats Ophelia-like upon the chilly, pimpled surface, another pretty leaf adrift upon the stagnant pool. One man on his bike slows to cycle round and round the limestone face of the circular fountain, somehow avoid the gawking walkers in his path, his eyes hungry for the imagined spectacle within the breathy, narrow arc of his repetitious ride. Content, we relish our cup's last delicious drops, cheered by the lively tints and airs of a dying season, the generous nature of this Indian summer weather, this unscheduled stir of our ageing senses. We wonder aloud why these two ventured here today: photos for a groom, for web or magazine, for fun, a dare, while shyly she averts her shining eyes from all but him, pretends we simply don't exist, we fading older ones. She shivers, wraps her goosey youth in woolen shawls, he gathers up his bulky working gear, they stroll away. We sit contented then. Cups drained, we feel quite full, and thankful for the random gifts our lives provide.

Night Death at the Marina

Some form a line at dockside
while others hug the rail above,
near the Marina office.
Some sit against the fence,
their fingers in the cool grass
as though it were a loved one's hair,
nervous family and friends.
All are facing south, waiting.
Out on the floating docks,
the divers and the police,
the firefighters and staff,
peer in silence into the water
below where they stand,
their thoughts peering up
toward them from deep down
within the murky depths
of the flowing, tidal river.
His friend had covered him
with a blanket that other night.
He'd fallen asleep on board
the cabin cruiser, after a few
too many drinks and laughter,
familiar stories, memories
of growing up in a small town.
Sometime through the night,
home called to him perhaps,
or, body urged him to get up.
He stumbled out and fell
into the airless, icy wet,
in the pitch black night,
got snagged below a dock,
or clothing weighed him down,
none of us will ever know.

But it ended for him there,
near where they found him
all those lonely hours later...
Soon for the waiting others
the hurt begins in earnest.

Judith Ann Smith
—In response to Bruno Bobak's Wheel of Life

He hadn't thought of her
in months.
No rueful backward
looks, no penitential
shedding of self,
no kneeling at the headstone
of their long buried love
in the bone yard of youth,
leaving to others
the gleaning of their story
from such scant statistics
as the births and deaths
on the mossy faces
of pocked and faded stone
in the neglected cemeteries
they liked to wander
warm Sunday afternoons.
Let others analyze
the short fiction
of their learner marriage,
that slow, revealing
process
of discovering
who they really weren't.
Watching their naïve
shades of green
bleed to faded bone.

He mentioned parting.
The stroke was cruel.
Her hurt slammed her
to the floor.
Surprised him.
Seared like white-hot lead.
And so they blew apart.
Bits of themselves
buttered the landscape,
staining everyone they knew,
while their souls
tried to die.
But still they lived
and with passing time
signs of hope returned:
she found a good man
more suited to the life
she always dreamed to live,
and he found love
strong enough
to hold his devils down,
and years slipped by.
They spoke from time
to time and did their best
with kids, on friendly terms
always and fair.
                    And then,
one day somewhere past
the expected middle
of her time, he learned
how she was gravely ill
and nothing could be done
but say good-bye.

Their children at her side
she swallowed
noble death in days,
and was no more.

      Deep inside him
something stirred,
and darkness
dropped
down
hard.
      Pools dammed up
behind his eyes,
and broke,
and dried.
Looking back,
her phantom face
pillared him
in salt.
He saw
the way she'd
been when love
was fresh,
and all of that
was dead except
their two strong sons,
and a thousand
small regrets.

Through This Rain (11 for November)

1. The Old

Halloween night; Aunt Aletha, lungs riddled with cancer, falls off the side of her bed and cries out in pain. Eighty-four years old, recent recipient of a replacement hip, she lies, uncomplaining, while two paramedics try, time and again, to start an intravenous in her fragile arms. Emergency service at the local hospital is closed temporarily, so she rides thirty rough miles in the speeding ambulance, and waits among masked H1N1 patients in the city. X-rays show no new damage, other than obvious bruising around her metal parts, so they ship her back to Perrin's Marina Villa. In the morning she jokes with us, despite her pain. Later, my friend Pete and I visit her huge old house, rich in family history. We pore over dozens of hand-written journals, more than a lifetime of days, pages cracked and yellow that speak of weather and ships, cargos and destinations long gone, year upon year of ordinary living reduced to flowing cursive lines. We exchange poetry books, and I uncork the Dalwhinnie. We toast the smooth and bitter of our swiftly passing days; savor the glow, the aftertaste…

2. Aletha

I see her there on the floor,
light as last summer's leaves,
arms and legs parchment wrapped twigs,
eyes alert, focused and resigned,
her voice clear, aware and as intelligent
as when I first knew this hard-smoking aunt,
who never wasted a word, or a moment,
on complaints, or idle gossip.
Hers was never an easy life,
but an existence full of good humor,
frank, practical, getting things done.
When her air force husband died
after many years of fighting M.S.,
she told me how much harder life
had suddenly become for her,
and I didn't understand. All that care,
all that looking after, and worry, and now
she was at long-last free of it all.
But here in her room at Perrin's,
waiting for the ambulance ride,
I'm seeing my own life in new ways,
and that of this woman, who has raised
her family, tended her invalid husband.
Her care of them was THE act of love,
and when they had gone away,
and she was left all on her own,
her house became an empty cave
full of ghosts, silence, and pictures of ghosts,
emptied even of the memory of echoes.
Her treasure the echo of remembered voices
in her active and impatient mind.

3. Growing Backwards

This afternoon at 2:00, I take my Aunt Aletha to see Doctor Johnston. Her children live many miles from here, in another province, and Aletha's car sits unused outside Perrin's Marina Villa, the senior's village, where she lives in a small room. Soon after she moved there, dehydrated, she became confused; demented, they called it, and her children worried about the car keys she carries in her carefully guarded purse. They can't be here to drive her to the doctor, who will decide if she can keep them, and so I will go, pretend I don't know. I've been here before, years ago with my mother, and I already mourn what we both may lose, this afternoon at Doctor J's.

4. Early Morning Phone Call

We're packing our bags for Saint John.
We'd written a different screenplay than this
a few short weeks ago: another grandchild,
laughter and joy, abundant celebration.
Instead, our son called and his love is covered
in warm blankets in the hospital, labor has begun
and it's premature. He has little hope
and we are going there to console or to grieve.
Zahra, their first, has been anticipating the new
like all first children do, with mixed emotions,
and her parents are devastated at this latest news.
They've been warned to expect the worst,
and we're bursting with the love that's burdened
by the present burning in our guts and minds,
and anything we say means nothing right now.

5. Saint John's Wort

We start out in driving rain,
mixed with snow,
gale force winds,
water pooled on pavement
—hydroplaning a concern
to add to our woes.
Son's wife about to miscarry
a long-sought-after second child.
She is in hospital in Saint John,
and we will see to Zahra,
much beloved first grandchild,
and allow Andrew to visit
with Melanie in the hospital.
We arrive safely and greet
one another, chins held high,
to try not alarm the child
who clings to her Papa's legs.
And for ourselves, disappointed,
we need to brew up protection
to fight those bitter juices
that have invaded our bellies.
After Papa leaves and Zahra is at play,
we think of Tipton's Weed,
St. John's Wort, hypericum,
herbal relief that solves nothing
but temporary anxiety, panic
spurred by the inevitable,
the unchangeable, a familiar part
of the mixed formula that is life.
The sun shines bright outside,
the storm has had its day,
and Zahra has gone to the park,
to write happy words in chalk,
where her grandmother is drinking in
her wort of healing, frequent laughter.

6. Should We Go Home For Now

This morning's light
crept softly through our window
from a soft grey sky.
Zahra woke and played quietly
in the room she shares
with Dora the Explorer,
most of the extra space
claimed by her pretend friend's
castles and belongings.
Pinks and pastels
wash the sharp edges
somewhat from her life.
She is singing now,
still thinks there will be
a new baby in the house.
The parents wait in hospital,
where they have been told
not to hope for happy outcomes,
but Zahra has been spared
such hard news for now.
Today the doctor comes
and they will form a plan,
and we will then decide
to stay here for a while
and be what help we can,
or head for home and wait,
do what must be done back there,
worry from a distance,
and when the end of time
arrives for all of this,
to bring our love back here.

7. The Slippery Nature of Isms

We are still in Saint John waiting for word from the hospital. Zahra has been dropped off at Prince Charles School, and we've slipped away from our responsibilities for a few moments. We're sitting at Cora's Restaurant where they serve great breakfasts, and I've ordered porridge, and multi-grain toast, Sandra, a strawberry Panini, with lots of whipped cream, and we both have coffee. Then cousin Philip phones from home, Prince Edward Island, and tells us Aunt Aletha is in the hospital again. She fell twice since we left. We tell him why we are here, about losing our grandson. There is silence on his end. He didn't know, of course, that we weren't home, or about our problems here. He says they'll pray for us. I thank him, don't mention how prayer is something I don't often do these days. My childhood was a blur of isms, and like Aletha most of them have slipped, and fallen, and I can't get to them from here.

8. This Is a Love Song for Henry Andrew

This is a love poem
for my grandson, Henry Andrew,
who was born last night
and lived, I suppose,
for a few moments,
outside the comfort
of his loving mother's womb.
And this is a poem of love,
for my thoughtful son Andrew,
and his lovely and intelligent wife Mel,
who hoped and dreamed of this birth
for several dozens of long months.
And this is a love poem for Zahra,
who wanted a baby, a sister or brother,
to play a thousand games with her,
and to sing, and run and laugh with her
on weekend mornings, and weekdays
after school is done all winter long,
and fifteen loving summers in the sun.
And this is a song of love
for my sensitive and dreamy wife Sandra,
who has loved every child she has ever met,
and every child who has ever lived,
even the short-lived babies of dreams
who weigh less then a dozen ounces
and have hand and footprints
no larger than the nails on her fingers.

9. Our Recent Emergencies

Recently our happiness found itself
sandwiched between two tragedies:
top slice, a miscarried, yearned for child,
bottom slice, a beloved, aging aunt,
whose lung cancer branched into her brain.
The bitter sandwich made palatable,
and sometimes fleetingly delectable,
as we played and laughed with, and at,
the antics of our blissful granddaughter,
who wanted a new baby to play with,
as yet oblivious to the tense drama
that occupied her grieving parents,
and had brought us, upset, to their home.
A sandwich garnished by visits to my aunt,
who we'd never gotten to know well
in all the years she'd lived nearby.
And we learned how sweet and kind
she is, and she'd become our forthright friend.
All this has emerged from a dual emergency,
a pair of misfortunes, beginning as crisis,
one now ended in tragedy, the second
sure to end the same in the coming weeks.
Time will bring its standard remedies:
the young marrieds will likely try again,
and perhaps there'll yet be a child or two.
If not, their family will grow in love
for the merry child they have, and one another.
With my cousins, we will weep to see Aletha go,
and she will help us through it all,
in each and every way she can. Memories
will wet and sting our eyes a little while,
and even these will turn more sweet
and fleeting as months and years go by.

10. Twelve

We spent twelve minutes in the hospital room visiting Aunt Aletha. We arrived and found signs posted warning us not to take a step inside without gowns and gloves. We don those, and masks; look like Halloween surgeons, see uncertainty, panic and fear in her cancer drained eyes. My memories flood back: thoughts of mother's final months, difficult days leading to the endless vigils before her drawn out parting, twelve short years ago. Aletha tears at a gauze bandage tied across a plastic intravenous port she's been anxious to yank out, as we explained a dozen times she should not do; she'd bleed and it would hurt her, as nurses probed her rolling veins when they struggled to fix her up. But she could not stop herself, her frown set in pure frustration. A dozen years she's lived alone, and today's lively, mixed-up roommate thrives on constant, mindless chatter my aunt cannot shut out. What remains of earthbound time is now confused and rather pointless, as she is packed and ready to leave. She is a women of simple religion, and her long-dead husband waits with a dozen of her siblings in a place she has yearned for, these many dozen days and nights, and she is and has always been an impatient and practical woman.

11. Waking Aunt Aletha

This morning cousin Nancy
finds her mother Aletha sleeping;
as my funny, palliative aunt does
so much, these past few weeks.
She hadn't touched her breakfast,
and even when she is awake
the spark has gone from her eyes.
One of them is permanently dilated;
systems are clearly shutting down.
Nancy and the ever-cheerful doctor
wear yellow throw-away gowns,
blue gauze masks, and rubber gloves
as they stand beside the dozing woman
in her rumpled bed. Her bruised legs
bare, she has removed her sweat pants,
part of some demented scheme
to finally free herself from this place.
Lung cancer has spread to her brain
and affects how she thinks and feels.
Doctor Johnston's bright voice calls,
"Aletha, can you hear me? It's me,
Doctor Johnston. Are you awake?"
She repeats herself several times more;
smiles patiently at the worried Nancy.
Finally, Aletha stirs in her bed
but her fading eyes stay closed tight.
"I'm dead," she says matter-of-factly.

Next morning she appears to be sleeping
as daughter Nancy looks at her.
Then, "Take me to the graveyard," she says.
Why would we do that? Nancy asks, unnerved.
"Figure it out for yourself," then she chuckles.
Death comes peacefully a few long days later,
her family gathers with much tears and laughter.

Life Measured Out in Blueberries

Late in the summer
we bought our blueberries.
Scoop after scoop,
we stowed them in bags
in our basement freezer
beside the beans and bread,
the strawberries, the carrots,
the peas and the cauliflower,
the Brussels sprouts,
and all the other frozen bits
lying in wait for the long winter.
Now day by day we measure
out our lives in blueberries,
a quarter cup at a time,
across the mixtures of bran
and oats, the müesli and granola,
the cold white milk.
These mornings we light the fire,
build upon the coals of the day before,
clear a path for air through the ashen grate,
open wide the draughts,
pile on the dry kindling
—old shingles from summer construction,
bits of branches from trimming
hedge and deadfall, dying trees—
then the precious beech, maple and birch.
We fill the kettle from the sink,
water from our own pure well,
and set it rocking on the stove
above the snapping flames,
drop a teabag in the pot,
ready the bowls and cups,
the spoons, and set the table.

The Day Before the Storm

The day before the storm
the lawn lay green as summer,
the morning sky bloodshot, wary.
And then on New Year's Eve,
the blast hit hard past midnight.
We crept home blind by 1:00,
and warmed up in our bed;
celebrated new and parting year
in our comfortable ways.
Morning brought a different world
beyond the icy, crusted windows,
across the lacy, crystal net of drift,
knee-deep carvings shaped by stroke
and cut, by swirl and howl of wind.
Only the white capped river waves
recall what was, one distant day before.
We sit safe in our warm rooms
as the world shifts and storms:
the radio speaks of war, death,
the new year's first-born child,
a boy gone missing in the storm,
(later found frozen under snow),
the tick, the tock, the freeze, the thaw,
cycle on cycle, as our seasons crawl,
then walk, then run toward the end.

Sorting Bent Nails

Today the snow glides down
winding slopes of still, cool air.
It softens the outside world
like a shroud of fine lace.
I am staying close to home
in spite of places I should go,
head stuffed up and weary,
a fine excuse to rest my bones,
pick at some chores, and write
a phrase I've carried in my head
and didn't want to bury
in my pillow or misplace
among the bent nails I meant
to straighten, or that plastic thing
I know belongs to something
precious we, perhaps, still own.

Three Crows

Minus 23 degrees Celsius.
The sun sits atop the dark spruce
on the eastern edge
of the river boundary.
It cuts through the bitter cold.
It bites, makes me squint.
Along the ice-locked river,
the shadows point to the northwest,
the deck, freeze-dried and bare,
the lawn lost under a blanket
of sugar-fine, frozen snow.
Before we head away to sing
at the white church on the hill,
I pull the hot pan of wood ash
from below the glowing fire grate
and lift the green compost pot
from beside the kitchen sink.
Outside I stop and blink my eyes
against the blinding winter light,
ash and compost toted in opposing hands,
walk the crusted face of the white lawn.
Three crows invade the sky above me,
swing down among the stark trees.
One carries something the other wants;
they attack and repel with reckless abandon.
Oblivious to my spellbound presence,
they soar and swoop like warring Spitfires,
momentarily astound, then disappear.

On Valentine's Day

Without these, your eyes,
would I have ever found love?
So much of what I feel
began with that first glimpse,
the lifting of the heart,
the intake of breath.
I have felt the energy
of your ardent look,
the touch of your mind,
that sets invisible fingers
to playing tabla within my chest,
the surrounding air full of energy,
oh so warmly breathing on my skin.

Walk in the Woods—Head of Montague

Home from Church and Allister waits.
He's made another trip to Lyndale
while we stood to sing our hymns,
and now suggests we come and view the trails
he's been breaking through our woods,
where he plans to build a straw bale house
somewhere near the stream, amid the trees.
We drive out there in separate cars,
so he can later head for work and home.
We stop a little past the last farm's gate,
then crunch slowly up the unplowed road
to where a narrow entrance spans the ditch
into our large plantation of larch, pine and fir.
We stumble up a path defined by pink ribbons
that dance in the wind on thin branches of tamarack,
and the serpentine hard-packed tracks of snowshoes.
We are careful not to stray from the narrow trail,
and sink into knee-to-thigh deep snow,
all around us signs of the invisible wild,
birds who speak in lovely foreign tongues, and
common crows and screeching gulls that drift inland
ahead of the latest storm, not fooled by bright sun
and endless blue of sky. The white ground littered
with abandoned paw prints, the corklike droppings
of the snowshoe hare, and feathery angels
brushed in blood-stained snow by the night-visioned owl,
the run and leap of the red squirrel, the swift stealth
of the coyote-worried and wary silent fox.

Now the ground slants downward and we continue,
down the slippery bank to the shallow stream
that cuts this land into two large snowy chunks,
its low valley and steep walls the safe harbour
for massive ancient hemlock spared by their size,
already huge enough back then to warrant awe,
when Europeans first began to chew up trees
for profit, heat, and to clear this million acre farm;
saved too by the terrible haul up the slanted slopes
when there was easier wood to hew and split
much closer to the season's hearth and home.
We pause a moment, listen to cold stream water
brush past the ice along its melting banks,
then turn and climb three hundred years to home.

Sunday Crossing

In the warm flurry of after church,
we graze through a light Sunday lunch
and watch through glass as granular snow
draws lace curtains across the landscape.
We dress then, scamper down steep riverbank,
carefully navigate icy sandstone steps,
out where snow-clad river ice awaits the spring.
Frozen puddles of melt ice appear here and there,
dot its face like tiny lakes of open water,
but strong enough, Sandra thinks, to hold us
after many weeks of unrelenting freeze.
We step gingerly along on full alert
as crisp snow compresses underfoot,
forms thin slabs that dart abruptly
as tiny sleds on snow-blanketed ice,
slick as oil or grease on burnished steel,
urging us to march lined up like penguins.
Suddenly solid-seeming melt-water ice
shatters underfoot and we drop an inch
through layered salty wet to thicker ice beneath.
Our hearts dart about like startled fish,
rise tight up against our lungs. I imagine
the speedy current close below our boots
drags our startled bodies into airless dark,
across the abrasive underbelly of the ice.
Happily we agree to turn around mid-river
and hurry home to where our solid house,
set in warm safety among the frosted trees,
has never seemed so lovely as now.

Precious Blood

Our snowy Sunday stroll ends at Gahan House,
the former Sisters of the Precious Blood Convent
whose cloistered nuns once manufactured disks
of altar bread destined to take on sacred flesh.
Wafers the boy imagined cut from starched wimples
that framed those silent women's exiled faces,
now long spent and swept aside like fallen leaves
after lives of contentment and postponed joy,
replaced today by slim waitresses with silver bangles,
and shiny hair, who distribute modern sacraments:
three-cheese pasta in square bowls, designer ales,
girls with bright eyes, who serve us well, collect tips,
unaware of those thousand hopeful, forgotten brides
whose dreams began once earthly days were done.

Spring Snapshot

All that day
the snow geese
winged their way north,
announcing to all below
that winter's back was broken.
But her foul breath
still chilled
our island bones.
The last of the dark snow
melted all day
in the high places,
and water danced its way down,
home to the St. Laurence
sometimes in a trickle,
sometimes in torrents
cutting rapids down riverbanks.
We watched a lively flow
cascade through rocks,
flood the gravel below
just above our hotel,
when David and I
went out walking,
dressed for early spring,
with Joe dressed for winter,
he and David squatted
beside the tumbling water,
atop a throne of granite,
Joe like a Russian dancer,
arms crossed upon his chest,
his face shivering out a broad grin,
beside him David in leather jacket
and Blue Jays cap,
his polished leather shoes
tucked under him,
smiling like a happy schoolboy.

Empty Houses

We leave our car before Cardigan Bridge; walk across and up the riverbank a way, before us a modern family house, and a lone tree, gaunt, barren, and tall, and through whose branches we see excited children who come here in cars, wave sticks, and skate gleeful circles between a pair of hockey nets, bathed in gilded sunlight that paints its gold on the silver face of the frozen river. The village is full of large, Sunday-best houses, all faced in wood, dressed in edible paint, toffees and lemons, chocolates and creams, up high on hills, on short, dead-end streets, safe places where traffic seldom goes now, constructed by crafters of fine wooden ships, powered by nature's persistent raw winds whose plaintive moans chill aging parents lodged in quiet rooms with large windows, built to watch for sailors, but now gazed through wistfully by those who long for gone away children, who in their distant and separate lives frantically struggle to build already empty houses.

Headache

Sometime through the night, the cat
jumps off a table or a kitchen countertop
downstairs and lands with a solid thud,
enough of a noise to wake me up
only marginally alarmed. I listen then
and hear his comments to some creature
on the other side of the glass, a growl,
or a seductive message too subtle for me
at that hour, and I drift off until the light
from outside peels away night's blankets
and the clock tells me I have enough time
to get downstairs, feed the cat who growls
in language I have heard before—he's hungry—
and prepare breakfast for sleepy Sandra
and myself, before heading for an oil change
up the muddy lane and ten miles up the road.
We eat our All Bran and drink our tea, talk
about how March has ended, and April
fools who will try to catch us with jokes.
I drive to Albion to the garage, and
do crypto-quotes and crossword puzzles,
and listen to others waiting for cars
talk about the weather and the economy,
and bailouts, and greedy thieves in banks,
and automobile manufacturing, and taxes,
the people with nothing much to gain who
will hand over most of their earnings to the rich,
who will find new ways to fill their pockets,
and throw away all the rest of it before
it gets wasted on health care, or education.
I pay the bill and drive quickly home,
my mind tied up in knots and barbed wire.

We take a long walk in afternoon sunshine,
and afterwards stop to buy a small Greek pizza,
before we head home, and reheat macaroni
and cheese we eat together, hoping to make
my blistering, hard-earned headache
fade enough so I can practice my solo
for choir practice this evening, at the church,
and Sandra smiles and kisses me until the sun
comes out and warms my ice cream headache mind,
and all those who-gives-a-damn shadows melt,
the way I always do every time she holds me.

How It All Begins

In the morning I awake
and read the time
from the clock radio to my left.
I view the sky in the window overhead,
check for snow, or rain,
blue sky and cirrus,
all of it exciting.
I turn to watch Sandra sleep.
I yawn, and I smile,
often find myself humming
a song, a hymn perhaps,
or a bawdy ballad,
as I roll off our bed.
I check the temperature
inside the room and out,
the thermometer a gift
of love from our children.
We pull back the drapes
to see how the wind plays
across the trees, and the passing river.
I look for crows, and songbirds,
or the soaring bald eagle
who loves to top the tall white pine,
ducks or geese that swim out front,
or a seal or two at rest upon the ice.
We eat and sip hot tea in silence
as we ride time's spinning wheel,
aware of each irreplaceable moment,
every moment's infinite possibilities.

Those Rolling Seasons

I remember that riverbank.
We sat in long grass,
our legs dangled
down the sandy bank,
and moonlight danced
across the pulsing water.
The back of my neck
buzzed like a purring cat,
and I was afraid to move
for fear of breaking the spell.
I remember that sidewalk,
and the feel of your ribs
beneath your summer dress
under my proud fingers,
your closeness as we walked,
the silent anticipation of night.
I remember our baby's cries,
his sudden bathroom delivery,
our joy and our laughter,
the doctor's late arrival,
all those rolling seasons,
years that pass like days,
our constant changing,
our accelerating joy.

Unwinding

Two nights ago,
in spite of bitter cold,
and well past sunset,
I carried my dusty driver
out onto our frosty deck,
and set an imagined ball
on its non-existent tee.
Carefully I looked off
into the darkness over the river,
while still, and shooting stars
looked down on me perplexed.
I addressed that waiting orb,
and placed my solid club face
perfectly beside, my muscles
slightly tensed, and anxious,
then low and slowly turned,
and lifted all that power up,
to circle round me there,
a Titanic deity of golf,
then let it go, and all unwound,
came speeding to the waiting ball,
which blasted to its perfect orbit
down the fairways of the sky.

Mid-April Morning

All is brittle as I step out
onto the frosted boards
of the deck, breathe
air's clean sharp edges.
The orange light is
thin, diluted where it
falls across last year's
yellow timothy.
In the bed down front,
between me and
the cumulus smudged
face of the river,
spruce-crowned
on the far shore,
close huddled crowds
of blue crocus shiver
in their icy beds,
stand and watch me
scan the paler blue
of the sky above.

Frosty Walk

Sunday morning early, we rise. There are bags to pack, after church we drive to Saint John, to help repaint a house slated for expropriation. We hope to raise the payout, before it gets torn down and the ground leveled. We load our car and walk up to the garden field, cover a wide circle, amid ten-foot spruce, and occasional, frost-tipped pine. It should be warmer now this late into the spring. We long for the sun's heat, we want to feel more warmth instead of the frustration and anger in our son's house, our anxiety for all of them, man and wife and all those cherished animals: the dogs, and cat, the chatty parrots, rescued from poor nutrition, owner's ignorance and neglect. But average weather means just what it says, there are always frosty days; and sometimes the perfect house simply stands in someone's way, and nothing we do can save it. So we'll give in with a smile, put on our warmest sweaters, take out the brushes and paint, and do what we can do.

Unlocking Spring

Last patch of winter's snow
in the north garden,
my spring heart blossoms.

How I Say Goodbye to April

At 2:30 your radio plays softly,
telling you the time has come
to gather cameras and gear,
and drive to North Lake,
record the first setting of traps
for this year's lobster season.
I listen to your morning sounds,
then house door, and car door,
engine, reversed transmission,
and your departing Doppler.
Restless and groggy, I lay there awake,
until just around 4:00, when I hear
the first fully loaded Cape Islanders
race and rumble down the wide river
from Montague to drop baited traps
onto the best possible bit of shoal.
This is how I say goodbye
to the joys and pains of April,
this signals the approach of summer;
not the melting of incessant snow,
nor the rotting of the river's thick ice,
not the cheerful throaty song of robins,
but this 4:00 am race down the river,
brief wakening, and dropping back to sleep.

Annual Photo Show

Charlottetown

The gallery is abuzz: photographers, families, friends, a score of curious supporters, all gathered to view hundreds of wall-mounted photos, to find out which the judges say are best. A few hungry regulars focus on mid-room tables: plates of savories and sweets, cheese and crackers, punch, while most focus on the photo-laden walls, or the side table where the ribbons and trophies await their presentations. One of three judges speaks first, praises the quality of the work, its improvement since his last judging. Then prizes are doled out, applause and photos, smiles and laughter, and, of course, barely hidden disappointment. But the walls tell the real truth. They present an edited world, shadowed highlights discovered on an extended walk down a frozen, deserted beach at dawn, or lively light bounced off white stone in the shades of a ghostly grave yard; inspiring light in an empty cathedral cavity, where sun, water, land and sky, tint the light filtered through patterns of stained glass; morning-lit mountains; solid, handsome gorillas; then, early morning in a well-lit harbour, with trap-laden boats tied up at rest, later, racing out the gap. Everywhere precious moments stopped, frozen replays of fickle, transient beauty, a sensual potluck feast of visual treats that leaves the eye stuffed and overfed as we drive home to carry on our lives, and recall bite by bite each morsel that we've seen.

The Lightening of Thin Cloud

We rise at 6:00 before the sun,
to the drum roll of pelting rain,
and threat of wet snow to come.
We head off without breakfast,
this the ritual morning when
Christ's diverse tribes gather,
with other seekers of the light,
on the dark fisherman's wharf
to greet the Easter rising of the sun.
Some come, fervent believers
in their literal, historic gospel,
the unalterable word of God,
others, drawn by the warmth
they feel from assumed teachings
of Jesus, the human son of man,
some who find truth in myths,
or skeptics fueled by optimism,
full of hope for something better,
coming to witness this latest "rising"
of our jaundiced mighty star.
This pale morning's sunrise
is the lightening of thin cloud;
a sun who scarcely warms at all.
Yet still we gather and rejoice,
we laugh and chat, and share a meal,
unsure perhaps how to explain
why we're called to gather here,
in search of something lost,
or buried deep inside of us,
our common joy in human life,
in all our hearts a "Christ within",
who rose in us with sleepy heads
to share the wonder every morning is.

Empty Handed

5:20 on a Tuesday
— outside my window,
not a single star
lights the velvet night,
my flawed heart
beats its sixty beats,
the metronomic magic
of generic Metoprolol
pushes the even flow
of my lonesome blood.
I wish I knew how
to cure the world
of sadness forever,
to share
—each time it's needed—
the simple joy I've felt
holding your warm hand.

The Shape of You

At first you were scraps
and fractals of form.
I would sleep and dream
fragments of laughter,
part of a smile, a glimpse
of your parting heels,
the fabric of a skirt.
Through time there whirled
a kaleidoscope of fractured forms,
a myriad of colors, gradually
slowing and settling into
momentarily stable shapes,
lines, curves, angles, slopes,
all in warm motion, attached
to a voice that in the same breath
calmed, and excited, a presence
which filled and emptied,
satisfied, and set me to craving,
never still but always constant,
as round and warm as the sun,
as cool and soothing as the moon,
a bed that never lost its comfort,
a roller coaster that never failed to thrill.

Dream

One night when I was old,
I felt you young beside me,
fitting my contours like
you were carved to lie there.
I knew I was alone
and such a dream belonged
in the lush green gardens
on the outskirts of imagination,
but I allowed the thought
to live a little while,
savouring the pictures
my tired old mind produced:
the firmness of our flesh,
the fullness of lip,
the fruity perfection
of your young breasts,
the citrus smell
of your perfect skin.

Blossoms

This morning opens warm,
the air soft with mist,
pink and white blossoms
thrust lush lips
into the world around,
yearn for the kiss
of air and insect,
the coming heat
of summer.
Inside,
burnt toast and coffee
wait in a yellow stone dish,
and a pair of chipped mugs
they have held a thousand
times. His strong arms sag,
and wrinkles underscore
her smiling eyes. Today
she will tend her flowers,
and he will paint the summer
chairs. They will sleep,
sometimes touching,
sometimes inches apart,
and like tender apple blossoms
will open to the world together.

Late Summer Renovation

Our old house rides the edge
of the ever-changing river,
like us it flows through time,
its worn wooden face endures
extremes of heat and freeze,
the kindness and cruelties of seasons,
that in time grind matter into dust.
It faces endless waves of moisture
that glisten wet or crystalline,
and eat away the thin, cosmetic
cloak of paint and tapered wood
to fibrous sponge that drinks water,
dries and rots, is tunnel-ridden home
to fat ants below double-glazed
windows gone foggy, dull, and grey,
seals spent, ledges sag and droop,
and we, too, are tired and getting old.
Time and tide erode our riverbank,
our wood and concrete steps
worn and broken, the even slope
of sculpted bank, where children
launched square-riggers into laughing summers,
all gone in the lapping slap of passing boats,
the anxious exhilaration of September storm.
But as the sun glows warm, we sit and talk,
together we resolve to take a stand,
and shore our shore in sandstone rock,
which may outlast us both we hope.
We plan a shelf where two or more
can sit and watch grandchildren play,
and there we sit and sip our tea and think,
content we know what we must do.

It's time we got to work on our old house,
to get some help and then to take the leap.
We pull down time-worn shingles nail by nail,
remove our purblind windows one by one,
then insulate and clad with timeless stuff.
The dark decay of cedar gone, no need to paint
on shaky ladders this bright vinyl stuff
we swore you'd never see on our pure house,
fresh windows gaze upon what's left of life.
From in or out, double-glazed, argon, low-e,
our house, now good as new, will see us out.

The Beating of the Drums

Everything begins sometime.
It's a Sunday morning,
breakfast constructing itself,
one giving orders to the other
who complies willingly. It is early,
and serving needs no planning,
no thought. The third, far younger
than the other bustling two,
in fact, their youngest son,
last of six, the lingering home child,
is standing in the shower, upstairs.
"Toast down!" she says and serves
the six-egg omelet cut three ways.
He steps across the room, retrieves
the toast, whole grain, and hot,
smelling of September, farm machines
that stir the dust filled air, the jam,
raspberry 2009, knifed from the jar,
the coffee poured, two cream, one milk,
two healthy hearts, one, its artery
blocked, but still a good old heart, she says.
They sit in sofas, chairs, the sun
warm and soothing, not hot like yesterday,
then up the lane they go all three to choir,
a special gift, he seldom goes to church,
the boy who leaves tomorrow for three months,
musician on the road, in charge of time,
the beating of the drums, the cymbal's crash,
its stirring ride counting off the seconds,
all those hi-hat minutes, hours, the days,
while they watch the clock, the lane, the mailbox,
and wait for moments half as fine as this.

Sometime Day or Night It Comes

There is this haunting quality to life,
the existence of certain uncertainties
that lurk somewhere waiting, ready.
Through the late summer and fall,
following a delightful month of August,
came a steady, unrelenting downpour
of rain, an absence of sunshine, fields,
acres of top-killed potatoes, of ripe beans,
up, and down along the road, turned to muck
impassable as the mire of Passchendale.
Farmers made bold attempts at harvest,
powerful tractors, heavy machines stuck
to the axles, equipment clogged, and useless.
Even after sun appeared, we watched the fields
along the road, straight potato drills shining,
pools of stagnant water clogging all the ruts.
How many thousands of rotting dollars
to add to all those farmer's endless woes,
to the depressing economics of recession.
Last Saturday, coming home from market,
I saw that all had changed, not a lone potato,
not a single blackened stalk of soy stood up
on any of those fields. Sometime day or night
great reapers came and everything had changed.
I felt relief, and the sunshine warmed me up
on that brisk, late autumn day. And yet,
I felt a sudden chilling somewhere deep inside
at how swiftly such despair can turn to untold joy,
and the most generous strings of circumstance
can, in the space between a breath, turn dark and grim.

Confederation Bridge, P.E.I.

At 80 kilometres per hour,
it takes 11 minutes to cross
its 13 kilometre span
across Northumberland Strait.
This gray concrete bridge
has solid cement walls
that prevent those in cars
from seeing the wide expanse
of water, or winter ice,
over which they pass
so quickly and with ease.
Atop the uppermost span,
comes a quick glimpse
of opposing shoreline, and
sometimes the rising or setting sun,
a floating raft of glistening ice,
or pristine whitecaps tossing
snowy foam on azure water...
much like how we steal brief moments,
to savor the splendors of our blind
journey across the span of years.

Butterfly House

In the Butterfly House,
all the butterflies
have damaged wings.
They are born here,
pupas suspended
on parallel bars,
like the arms of a rotisserie,
inside a closed box
with one glass side,
curtained so visitors
can peep inside,
view the intimacy
of their moist entry
into this the first
of their prisons,
the initial unfurling
of their magnificent wings.
Once dry,
they are released
into a deceptively
wider world,
the netted confines
of this glass house,
with its illusion of sky,
its blurred impressions
of enfolding wilderness.

Butterflies never eat,
but they drink here,
become intoxicated
on nectar and rotting fruit,
stand like tattooed
cardboard cutouts
on the heads and shoulders
of paying tourists,
beat their fragile wings
against wood and glass,
in their yearning
for some distant,
indescribable
destination.

Buying Flowers and Beer

...poems will not really buy beer or flowers
*or a goddam thing...*al purdy

Explosions of idea,
snapshots of beauty,
bursts of insight and colour,
howls of laughter, moans of pain,
blooms of love and friendship.
None born structured in sentence,
just swaggering word, or phrase,
fresh-hatched in the mind,
sometimes transferred to paper,
but mostly dead and buried
in the infertile soil of silence,
as I struggle to take part
in polite conversation.
In truth I take real joy
in filtering how I see the world
through the fibers of my brain,
hoping I might find the words
that best recall what I took in,
hopeful some other mind
will find artful worth in it,
perhaps discover there
something fine as flowers,
satisfying as ice-cold beer.

Construction

Did I begin with blocks,
pile them into lines
that tumbled and rolled
before they stood,
jagged as the walls
of ruined castles,
or bombed cities?
Or first, a concept, a crayon
tracking random marks
across the walls
of brown paper
grocery bags
from Highland Groceteria
down the street,
and round the corner
from my father's new house?
Or was it a tunneled drift
in our back garden,
or an igloo built
of shovel-cut blocks,
piled in shrinking circles,
or that underground fort
where we sat and smoked,
in the field below
Seaman's farm
or in the jungle
of apple and plum trees
behind Paul McGuigan's house?

Or the several houses since:
the rented basement,
the rented house in Montague,
Mr. Buchanan's wee renovated house
on Lampert Lane, the contracted house
on Cambellton Ave ,
the cottage I built in Brudenell,
or the final renovated cottage
we bought, raised up, and rebuilt
beside this constant changing river
that is our glorious life.
Like ants we construct our worlds
and the world erodes,
turns them back to earth,
and we build again and again,
until time sounds the final horn.
There are no stars for what we build,
the real reward is in the act of building.

Symphonic Noises

Yesterday the symphony,
a magical afternoon of Mendelssohn,
Elgar, Tomasi, and Burge.
This morning I awake
to a murderous fanfare of crows,
the riotous ruckus of geese
lifting from the security of mid-river,
as in the distance we hear the early morning
whump, whump of hunters in their blinds.
Over coffee, we read our novels
as wood snaps and roars in the grate,
fuels the kettle's steady hiss and bubble.
Outside, the percussive lap of rising tide
signals, at nine o'clock, the dueling moan
and growl of chain saws, the fall of tree,
the snap of breaking branches, the crash
that shakes the earth beneath my feet.
The rise and fall of the songs of saws
continues, until our neighbour's dying tree
is cut and neatly stacked in piles to burn.
Sandra is talking on the phone to someone
about some visits we will later make.
Then there is water, rinsing dishes in the sink,
the rattle and clink of metal on porcelain,
the glide and slide of drawer, the bang of door.
She stops when all is put away. Then sweet silence
and the kettle's steady hissssssssssssssssss.

About the Author

Poet, editor and novelist Hugh MacDonald of Brudenell is the new poet laureate for Prince Edward Island.

With nine books to his credit as author and editor, MacDonald is perhaps best known to Islanders through his Random Acts of Poetry which, for the past five years, have brought poetry to the streets and workplaces of P.E.I.

MacDonald retired after more than 30 years of service in the educational system of the province and, since 1999, has been a full-time writer. He has served on the executives of both the Prince Edward Island Council of the Arts and the P.E.I. Writers Guild. Recognition for his work and leadership includes awards and prizes in the P.E.I. Literary Awards including the L.M. Montgomery Children's Literature Award for Chung Lee Loves Lobsters, a first prize for poetry from the Writers Federation of Nova Scotia.

In 2004, he was presented with the Award for Distinguished Contribution to the Literary Arts on Prince Edward Island.